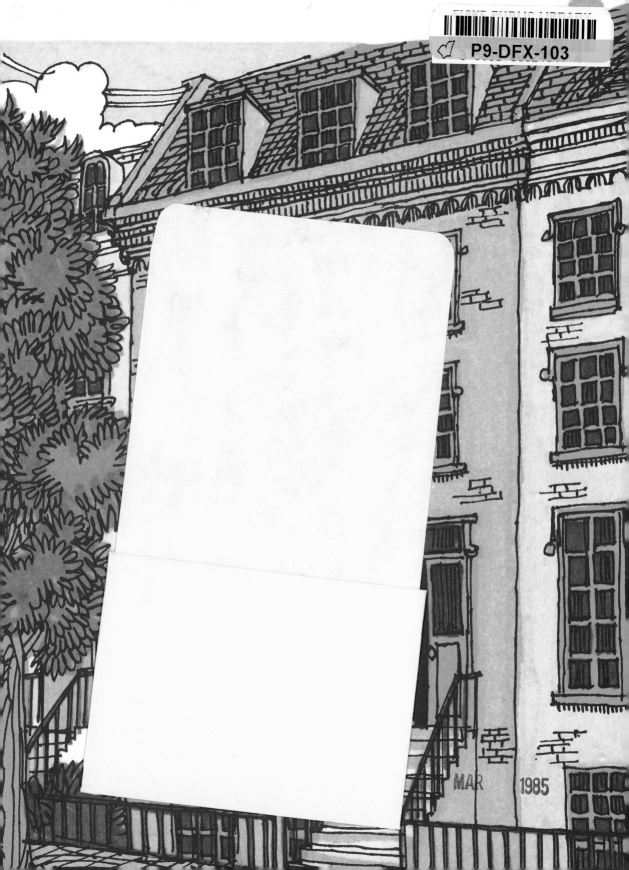

Robert Quackenbush

Don't You Dare Shoot That Bear!

A Story of Theodore Roosevelt

Prentice-Hall, Inc.
ENGLEWOOD CLIFFS, NEW JERSEY

Copyright © 1984 by Robert Quackenbush

Printed in the United States of America   ·J

Prentice-Hall International, Inc., London
Prentice-Hall of Australia, Pty. Ltd., Sydney
Prentice-Hall Canada, Inc., Toronto
Prentice-Hall of India Private Ltd., New Delhi
Prentice-Hall of Japan, Inc., Tokyo
Prentice-Hall of Southeast Asia Pte. Ltd., Singapore
Whitehall Books Limited, Wellington, New Zealand
Editora Prentice-Hall do Brasil LTDA., Rio de Janeiro

10 9 8 7 6 5 4 3 2 1

Library of Congress Cataloging in Publication Data

Quackenbush, Robert M.
  Don't you dare shoot that bear!

  Summary: A humorous biography of the twenty-sixth
president, emphasizing his love of animals and wildlife
and his activities as a conservationist.
  1. Roosevelt, Theodore, 1858-1919—Juvenile literature.
2. Presidents—United States—Biography—Juvenile literature. 3. Conservation of natural resources—United States
—History—Juvenile literature. [1. Roosevelt, Theodore,
1858-1919. 2. Presidents. 3. Conservationists. 4. Conservation of natural resources] I. Title.
E757.Q33 1984   973.91′1′0924 [B] [92]   84-4693

And with grateful appreciation to
Theodore Roosevelt Association

Theodore Roosevelt, or "TR" as he was to be called years later by an adoring public, was the oldest boy of four children. He was born on October 27, 1858, in New York City. As a child, he suffered from asthma, an illness that made it difficult for him to breathe and kept him very weak and sickly. Because he was confined to his bed so much during his childhood, TR was educated by tutors who came to the family house on Twentieth Street near Union Square. His favorite subject was science. And his favorite book was Livingstone's *Missionary Travels and Reaches in Africa,* a volume so large and heavy that he had difficulty in carrying it from room to room.

TR was determined to overcome his illness. When he was twelve, his father, a wealthy glass merchant, bought him a punching bag, a set of dumbbells, and other gymnastic equipment. TR set to work to build up his body and his muscles. As his health began to improve, he spent a lot of time outdoors and began collecting specimens for his own museum. He kept them in a case in a back upstairs hallway. He caught butterflies and beetles and mounted them. He learned how to stuff birds. Soon he had 250 different specimens—everything from minnows and salamanders to groundhogs and blue jays. To his mother's horror, his experiments included keeping a dead mouse in the icebox and live turtles in the washtub. Visitors to the "Theodore Roosevelt Museum" were charged a penny, but children were let in free—providing they helped feed the live animals.

10

Nature was not all that interested TR. He loved to read about Davy Crockett, Daniel Boone, and the brave cowboys in the West. He dreamed of becoming a cowboy himself one day. Then, in 1872, when he was fourteen, TR experienced firsthand a totally different part of the world. The family went to Egypt and wintered on a houseboat that coasted along the Nile River. TR kept notebooks and crammed the pages full with his observations and experiences. He also cleaned and mounted scores of native birds. The journey was the high point of his self-education in biology. Now he had gained enough information about birds and animals to astound professional naturalists.

When it came time to go to college, TR changed his mind about being a cowboy and a scientist. He studied history and law at Harvard and thought about being a writer. Some of his more reserved classmates were a little taken aback by his energy, his bouncy way of walking, his squeaky voice and funny way of talking. "That fellow with whiskers and glasses!" they would say. They were talking about the full sideburns TR sported at the time and the thick glasses he needed for his nearsightedness. They also thought he was odd because he kept his college room filled with stuffed birds and live lizards and snakes. But in spite of what his classmates thought, TR was an excellent student. He was curious and hardworking. He was proud when he made the college boxing team. He even began research, while a senior, on his first book, *The Naval War of 1812*. TR said years later that this book was "so dry that it would have made the dictionary seem light reading in comparison." But to educators it was a scholarly work.

15

Upon his graduation from Harvard, in 1880, TR married Alice Lee, an 18-year-old girl from Boston. They lived in New York, and TR began to think about his father's idea that men of wealth should devote themselves to public service. He decided to go into politics. He was nominated for State Assemblyman, one of the men who would make New York State's laws. A lot of people didn't think his "upper-class" ways would appeal to the voters. But TR knew how to relate to all kinds of people. And he particularly enjoyed a good fight. So he went out to campaign and he won! From 1882 to 1884 he was an assemblyman in the State Legislature in Albany, New York. He fought against corruption and unfair labor practices. He conducted an investigation of New York City government. And he fought to wipe out the city's slums and overcrowded living conditions.

16

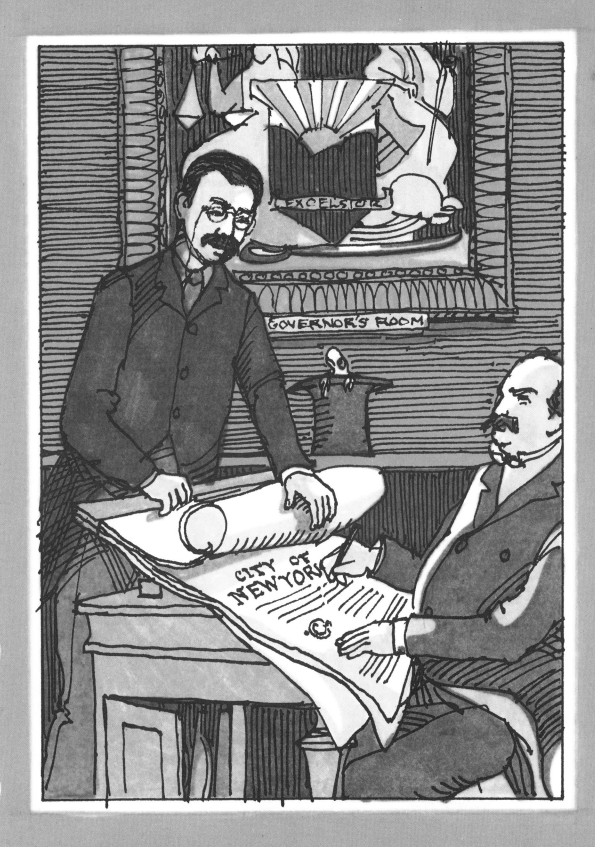

In 1884, while TR was serving his third term in the legislature, tragedy struck. His wife died after giving birth to a baby girl. Only a few hours later his mother died of typhoid fever. TR felt that his life was over. He finished his term in office, left his baby daughter in his sister Bamie's care, and headed West. He bought a ranch in Dakota Territory with money he had inherited from his father, who had died just a few years before. Out on the rugged prairies, TR's broken spirit began to mend. At last, he realized his boyhood dream of becoming a cowboy. The seasoned cowboys on his ranch had snickered when they saw the "City Dude" dressed in a over-sized sombrero, fringed buckskin shirt, and sealskin chaps. But they were surprised at how quickly TR became a first-rate cowboy. He worked right alongside them, roping calves and taming wild bucking horses. He even led a 100-mile chase and captured three thieves at gunpoint.

A year later, in 1885, TR returned to New York to see his baby daughter, who was named Alice after her mother. While there, he saw his childhood friend, Edith Carow. Soon he decided to return to New York for good. Edith and he were married and Edith became a loving mother to Alice. In the next few years, TR and Edith had five more children. TR supported his family by writing several books. They included *Hunting Trips of a Ranchman, The Wilderness Hunter,* and *The Winning of the West*. He also plunged back into political life. From 1889 to 1895 he served as a U.S. Civil Service Commissioner in Washington, D.C. He supervised certain government workers. Then, in 1895, he was offered the position of New York Commissioner of Police. In his ongoing fight against corruption, TR kept the police force on its toes. At night he would disguise himself in a black coat and slouch hat and go searching for any policemen who were neglecting their duties.

TR was Police Commissioner for two years. Then in 1897, when President McKinley took office, he was offered the position of Assistant Secretary of the Navy. TR gladly accepted. At the same time, a war with Spain was brewing. Rebels in Cuba and the Philippine Islands were already fighting to free their homelands from brutal Spanish rule. The Americans were on the rebels' side. Then on the night of February 15, 1898, the American battleship *Maine* mysteriously exploded in the harbor of Havana, Cuba. Many men went down with the ship. But McKinley was hesitant to declare war. TR was furious. One afternoon, when the Secretary of the Navy was away, he sent a cable to the commander of the U.S. fleet in the Pacific, telling him to keep watch on Spanish ships and to be prepared for war. Two weeks later, McKinley did ask Congress to declare war. And because of TR's cable, the American navy in the Pacific was ready. Ships sailed into Manila harbor in the Philippines and in a few hours routed the Spanish from the islands.

23

Eager to go off to war, TR quit the navy in 1898 and got permission to form a volunteer cavalry regiment, called the Rough Riders. He was to be Lieutenant Colonel of the unit. From all over the country, young men came forward to serve under him—cowboys and Indians, college boys, and even some policemen who had worked with him in New York City. TR said, "Give them great meals of beef, and iron and steel. They will eat like wolves and fight like devils." With that, TR took his men by ship from Tampa, Florida to storm Cuba. When the Rough Riders landed, reporters all over the world wrote about their bravery and told how they rode up San Juan Hill and captured it. In truth, the famous charge was not a "ride" as the reporters said. The regiment's horses had been left behind in Tampa. Only TR had a horse, which he rode only as far as a fence, where he dismounted. But walk or ride, TR and his men were rough on the Spanish. The war was over in a few weeks and the Cubans got their country back. "Oh, we have had a bully fight!" declared TR.

The Spanish-American War was reported in all the newspapers and TR was an overnight hero. Upon his return from Cuba, he campaigned for the office of governor of New York State, and won. Some of the politicians in Albany were unhappy about this. They believed that TR might weaken their positions in the state government. So they arranged to get him nominated for Vice President of the United States when it was time for President McKinley's re-election. McKinley won the election and TR went off to Washington. The political bosses heaved a sigh of relief. They knew that a vice president has no power unless he replaces the president in that officer's absence or disability. Then something shocking happened. In 1901, at the World's Fair in Buffalo, New York, McKinley was shot, and he died soon afterward. So, at 42, TR became the youngest president the United States had ever had. "A cowboy for President!" wailed the Albany bosses.

But TR fooled everyone. Not since Abraham Lincoln had the White House seen a president like TR. The United States was just emerging as a world power and needed his energy. It was America's good fortune that he was present to undertake the gigantic task of building a modern nation. He was all over the place, engaging in such causes as protection of working people, equal rights, a "square deal" for all citizens, pure foods and medicines, and conservation of our natural resources. Above all, he believed in honesty and fair play. In 1902, on a hunting trip in Mississippi, he refused to shoot a bear someone else in the party had stunned. When the story was published in the newspapers, TR captured the hearts and sympathy of millions. A toy bear was created and named after him. Today, the Teddy Bear remains the most popular of all children's toys.

28

During his years as President, TR always made sure he had time for his children. He played with them in the White House while important people waited to see him. He romped with them on the lawn of Sagamore Hill in Oyster Bay, Long Island—called the summer White House—where his family lived three months of the year. Edith never complained. She thought every house—even the President's official home—should be a relaxing place to live. In her efforts to make the White House comfortable, she got rid of the heavy Victorian furniture and bric-a-brac. She redecorated in a simpler, more classic style. And she arranged for Alice, the oldest daughter, to be married there. Alice was as famous and popular as any movie star we have today and even had songs written about her, including the classic "Alice Blue Gown."

TR became the most popular man in the nation. It is no wonder that he served two terms in the White House. People everywhere bragged about his "Big Stick" policy in international affairs and his "trust busting" at home. He arranged for the building of the Panama Canal. He negotiated a settlement of the Russo-Japanese War in 1905, which earned him the Nobel Peace Prize. But of all the things he did, his work as a conservationist is best remembered. He began his life as a naturalist and ended it as a naturalist and he never gave up his interest in wildlife. During his presidency, he created fifty-one national bird reservations, five national parks, four big game refuges, the first national game reserve, eighteen national monuments, and increased the area of national forests by more than forty-three million acres.

33

When his second term as president ended, TR went off on an expedition to Africa. It was sponsored by the Smithsonian Institution in Washington, D.C. Accompanied by his son Kermit, a team of scientists, and 260 porters and guides, TR's safari began. But this was not a luxury tour. Most of the porters were needed for transporting the equipment of the naturalists who were doing museum work. The year-long safari was the most successful specimen-collecting expedition of its time. The animals may still be seen today in the Smithsonian Institution in Washington, D.C. And after that trip was over, TR turned around and went on a dangerous mission for the American Museum of Natural History exploring a remote river in Brazil which became known as *Rio Teodoro*. When friends asked him why he was doing all this, TR had only this to say: "I have to go. It is my last chance to be a boy."

35

Epilogue

Theodore Roosevelt, 26th President of the United States, orator, statesman, historian, cowboy, explorer, hunter, naturalist, humanitarian, and philanthropist, believed that every person must do his or her own work. He emphasized that it didn't matter what one's position in life was: whether born to labor or luxury, action—intense action—was absolutely necessary. He was against anything lazy. It took him five years to rise from Police Commissioner of New York City to President of the United States. He wrote over 30 books, 150,000 letters, and countless articles and speeches. In a life of only sixty years, he lived to the fullest and as though each day was his last, for he believed that life is a precious gift. This belief was formed in childhood. As a sickly youth, he learned courage by overcoming fear, and strength by overcoming weakness. In his later years, he said, "In this world the only thing supremely worth having is the opportunity coupled with the capacity to do well and worthily a piece of work, the doing of which is of vital consequence to the welfare of mankind." This could be said of his whole life.